Spirit Living

Spirit Living
Abundantly Following Jesus

S. Robert Maddox

Spirit Living

Published by Redefining Faith Resources

ISBN: 978-0-98900-275-2
eISBN: 978-0-98900-276-9

DEDICATION

To the family of my heritage, the wife I love, the children I cherish, the grandchildren I adore, the friends I admire, the people I led, the Church Movement I respect and the Lord I serve.

Thank you for your love, your encouragement, your counsel, your support, your help and your trust. Following Jesus may be the road less traveled but is the only one filled with meaning and purpose. I am deeply fortunate and profoundly blessed.

CONTENTS

FOREWORD
"Get Ready..."

Bob has indelibly influenced my life as I sat regularly under his teaching for more than a decade while living in Chicago. When I had important questions, I often went to him and his answers constantly challenged me beyond my comfort zone.

Today, when I contemplate matters in my life, I can still hear his words cautioning me toward wisdom. One of the greatest I heed is, *"When making an important decision, ask your wife for her advice. She has the most at stake!"* This word of guidance has greatly influenced me, along with many others that have proven to possess staying power.

In this book and teachings you will be challenged to go beyond the surface and truly explore the topic of Spirit living. If knowledge is power, then the thoughts contained in these pages will help you be a dynamic force for God and His kingdom. Bob's insight in living as a follower of

Jesus will lead you to a lifetime of pursuing knowledge due to his lifetime of study. Get ready...

Ron DiCianni

TapestryProductions.com
rdicianni.com

PREFACE
"Before Starting"

For more than three and a half decades I was privileged to serve in church ministry. In the early years of *small beginnings* I had ample time to write and become published, an ambition of mine since childhood. For some unknown reason I was honored to provide leadership in prominent settings, leading an institution of higher education, leading in the church movement of my affiliation, including a couple of years on a national committee, leading on a few non-for-profit executive boards and leading two larger churches in the Chicago area. Writing for publication was suspended for a season but the desire to write remained strong.

The ability to devote time for creating articles and books has finally returned. Along with writing has come an opportunity to coach athletics. Besides being an ordained minister, I am a nationally accredited volleyball coach, helping students learn about life through a fast-action sport. When devoted exclusively to church ministry I regularly spoke about leadership at training sessions, specialty seminars and minister conferences. The same concepts are now being communicated to high school students, helping them to become *winners for life.*

I have been very fortunate and have had some amazing volleyball teams and winning seasons. Each match is different, never knowing what will be encountered and sometimes wondering if the team is ready for the challenge. Occasionally during a game nothing seems to go right. Serves are misdirected, blocks are missed, passes are off target, sets are poorly positioned, and hits are ineffective. When players are struggling with their mental game the encouragement in a sixty-second timeout is direct and simple: "Remember the fundamentals and do the basics. Get back into the natural rhythm of the game and work your way out of the momentary slump. Do the essentials with excellence and take back the winning edge." The teams through the years have given audiences some exciting finishes.

This book is about the basics of Spirit living and about finishing the course of life with excellence. Through intense struggles, honest questioning and earnest reflection the thoughts in this book have given me a life of joy and eternal anticipation. I am thankful for the privilege of following Jesus.

These teachings have been communicated to

several church audiences and a number of discipleship groups. While preparing for each presentation thoughts were further clarified and expanded. Continually reading Scripture and numerous publications as well as talking with associates enlarged and fine-tuned ideas. The book has been an ongoing lifelong endeavor.

The vast majority of references are Scripture. I believe every other source has been acknowledged, however, some may have been inadvertently missed or not remembered. Most quotes came from books of common sermon illustrations or were personally heard by speakers at various events. The definitions of the nine supernatural manifestations of the Spirit came from some long forgotten contributor, likely common domain. May the book give you reason to pursue more fully every blessing God has designed for you.

Bob Maddox

bob-maddox.blogspot.com

INTRODUCTION
"The Journey Begins"

My life is not a story of tragedy and abuse. My upbringing could hardly have been better - terrific parents, grandparents, siblings, and friends. A life filled with great experiences and wonderful adventures.

My parents had a measure of religious instruction but, as a family, we did not attend church. While possessing high moral standards Mom and Dad instilled beliefs rooted in established American traditions.

My father was an outdoorsman. August was spent each year boating and camping. We would boat the waters of Puget Sound in the Pacific Northwest, exploring the San Juan Islands and catching our food, mostly clams, crab and salmon. Teenage years involved camping the Canadian Rockies of British Columbia and Alberta, hiking mountain trails and keeping bears out of our campsites. He taught life in the wilderness and a love for natural beauty.

My mother was the sports enthusiast. She registered us for team programs offered by the Seattle Park District, partly motivated for personal private time. There was not a season or a sport omitted and nothing was optional. Our lives became enriched by competitive games.

Both parents loved music and gave us an appreciation for the arts. Everyone played musical instruments and enjoyed singing. Holidays and special occasions often involved musical performances by one or all.

My grandparents lived only a few city blocks from our house. My sister, brother and I had time with them weekly, usually for dinner and a television western, sometimes for swimming and picnic at a favorite lake, and occasionally to attend professional baseball games or all-star wrestling matches. They provided unconditional love and encouragement while growing up.

My sister and brother were an important part of my childhood. The numerous boating and camping trips required us to be playmates. Conflicts were many but our love was deep and our bond was strong.

My sister was the primary babysitter, a job she

did not enjoy. She was smart, pretty, ambitious and creative. She did not believe in God but was extremely compassionate and caring, much more than anyone I have ever known. She never stopped watching out for me her entire life and always helped, when needed.

My older brother was my roommate. The bedroom barely withstood the roughhousing and he won every wrestling match. No one ever gave me any hassle because of him, my unpaid protector. Unfortunately, he died early in life because of chemicals used in the Vietnam War.

There were many fun-loving friends, buddies keeping secrets, teammates laughing in locker rooms, musicians honing skills and reveling in tomfoolery, and classmates helping with schoolwork. Although we could occasionally be reckless, none were troublemakers nor intentionally caused harm.

I lived in a great city, nice neighborhood and wonderful home, surrounded by terrific people. Why did I feel empty? Why was I searching for answers to questions I did not know how to ask? Why did I feel lonely and afraid? Why did life seem boring and senseless? Something was missing! A hunger for answers kept gnawing at me and caused me to keep searching for purpose.

An attractive girl invited me to a church service during my junior year in High School. The church, an impressive worship facility, was well-established and fairly large. The property was well groomed, the vehicles in the parking lot were pricy and the people dressed in high fashion.

The Sunday morning service became the catalysis for a spiritual probe. The music was enjoyable and performed with excellence. The prayers were sincere and direct. The talk resonated with common sense.

Something unusual happened. In the balcony a person began speaking in an unknown language and someone else responded with an encouraging comment. The experience was not *frightening* but *mysterious*. A craving to understand the ways of God was birthed.

I began reading an unused Bible located in an upstairs closet at home and discovered biblical characters living with fears, mixed with faith. The book contained intriguing narratives about people with an uncanny sense of authenticity and about others living fraudulently.

After a couple months of reading and attending church, I decided to follow Jesus. The *search* converted into a *journey*.

Life took on new meaning. Outlook, interests and ambitions began to change. Some changes occurred quickly, others came slowly. A few unwholesome vises stopped immediately, others involved internal anguish and struggle. I wanted to understand why and how everything had become *different.*

After five years of following Jesus an additional experience enhanced the spiritual transformation. The Bible describes a baptism involving the Holy Spirit. Many had been encouraging me to seek this experience. Hours were spent at altars praying to receive what the Lord promised to every believer.

During a Sunday evening gathering a guest speaker invited everyone to come forward. He asked us to lift our hands and audibly praise God at the altar. Not expecting anything different, I found myself speaking in an unknown language, engulfed in the Acts 2 experience.

The journey was suddenly enhanced. Mannerisms went through additional adjustments and a resolve to tell others about Jesus intensified.

More is designed for believers than simply entering a personal relationship with God. Spiritual adventures await anyone willing to become totally engaged with Him. Signs and wonders are part of the journey. Believers have the privilege of accurately and fully representing God to the world.

Explore the journey God has established for followers of Jesus.

Jesus answered him, "Truly, truly, I say to you, unless one is born again he cannot see the kingdom of God."... Do not marvel that I said to you, 'You must be born again.' The wind blows where it wishes, and you hear its sound, but you do not know where it comes from or where it goes. So it is with everyone who is born of the Spirit." (John 3:3, 7-8 ESV)

For the death he died he died to sin, once for all, but the life he lives he lives to God. So you also must consider yourselves dead to sin and alive to God in Christ Jesus. (Romans 6:10-11 ESV)

That you may be blameless and innocent, children of God without blemish in the midst of a crooked and twisted generation, among whom you shine as lights in the world. (Philippians 2:15 ESV)

CHAPTER ONE
"Conversion"

What role does the Holy Spirit have in followers of Jesus?

People who place their faith in God are *pilgrims* passing through life. Life is a progression of inter-connected and sometimes overlapping events. Things achieved in the past prepare today; activities done today shape tomorrow. Life is never idle.

After making a decision to follow Jesus, life changed. My parents were raising me but the encounter with Jesus was changing me. What were the *why* and *how* of these changes? Does conversion involve only a change in destiny or does the experience continue making inner changes throughout a lifetime? I discovered conversion to be traumatic and gradual, instantaneous and ongoing.

Jesus referred to conversion as being "born of the Spirit" (John 3:8). Being "born again" gives *birth* to Spirit living. How does this impact life?

When the Apostle Paul wrote about the bodily resurrection, an analogy was given that applies to conversion. Answering a question about the resurrected body, he responded, "What you sow does not come to life unless it dies. And what you sow is not the body that is to be, but a bare kernel, perhaps of wheat or of some other grain." (1 Corinthians 15:36-37 ESV)

Death then life

"We have been united with him in a death like his ... our old self was crucified with him...." (Romans 6:5-6 ESV)

Crucifixion is a slow death. Someone on a cross is considered dead and is also dying. The old self is dead. "Therefore, if anyone is in Christ, he is a new creation. The *old has passed away*; behold, the new has come." (2 Corinthians 5:17 ESV) The old self is also dying. "*Put off your old self*, which belongs to your former manner of life and is corrupt through deceitful desires, and to be renewed in the spirit of your minds." (Ephesians 4:22-23 ESV) The nature that existed before conversion is *dead* and *dying*.

In conversion, like crucifixion, dying involves struggle. There is a struggle of *desire*. A personal desire to change, often caused by crisis, produces a search for solution. Crises include things like a souring marriage, a home in turmoil, addiction, physical health or personal safety.

A crisis can generate comments like, "I want to turn a new leaf ... wipe the slate clean ... start over." They can also create a realization that many problems are bigger than anyone can solve. Feelings of hopelessness develop.

A second struggle involves *determination.* Attempts are made to change through self-effort, sheer willpower. "I'll never touch another drop of alcohol ... I'll never be cruel to my family again ... I'll never...." Regardless how noble or resolute the intentions, problems reoccur and continue.

A third struggle involves *defeat.* Two facts become evident: 1) The inner core is imperfect, and 2) The human nature is incapable of producing genuine change. Reality can be brutal; truth can be hopelessly cruel. Everyone needs a Savior to save them from the human dilemma.

A fourth struggle involves *decision.* A crossroads has been reached requiring a resolve to press on or run away, submit or rebel, accept or reject. Without exception everyone faces this junction. Some mistakenly think rejection *creates* consequences yet people are *already* living with the consequences. John 3:18 states, "...whoever does not believe is condemned *already*...." The crossroads calls for a response, a place Ezekiel calls "the valley of decision."

Godly conviction sometimes reverts to self-condemnation. The Holy Spirit nudges the human heart to change and the person reacts by thinking change is impossible. No one is so bad that God cannot transform.

Desire, determination, defeat and decision; the nature of deadness is realized. Life becomes possible.

New and renewed life

Coming to life includes a sense of overwhelming newness. Old ways of thinking are incapable of comprehending the full nature of new life. Longtime friends find it difficult relating to new converts and new converts become increasingly uncomfortable doing past activities. Interests and desires change. The convert may not *feel* different but an eternal process has begun.

Consider a seed. Place the seed in the ground and unbury it the next day. The seed looks the same but an internal process has begun. If left in the ground change will eventually become visible and the stem will be very different from the seed. (1 Corinthians 15:36)

The convert is dead as well as dying, new and being renewed. The *new* is a different relationship with God; the *renewed* is being brought back to the original design by the Holy Spirit.

As Adam was before his rebellion, the convert is becoming by following Jesus. Before conversion the pure image and likeness of God was lost. Conversion is entering a pilgrimage back to what God originally intended. Before conversion prayer is a conversation with "The Creator;" after conversion prayer is a conversation with "Our Father." John 8:44 indicates before conversion the devil is father. This does not imply demon-possession; rather, people are more aligned with his nature. After physical death everyone goes to dwell with their *father*, the one they identified with in life.

In conversion the old nature dies and eternal life begins. A pilgrimage commences and renewal starts. The goal is *becoming like Jesus,* not *going to heaven*; heaven is the *destination.* Frustration develops when heaven becomes the goal instead of Jesus.

Completely lost

"Are you saved, brother?" What an odd question to an inner-city kid, raised in an all white neighborhood. I had been called "dude," as well as some unsavory names, but never "brother." I had a brother but he was not asking the question. What is this "saved" business?

Human nature is comprised of three

components: Intellect, Emotion and Volition. Every part of the human nature was tempted and impacted when Adam rebelled in the Garden of Eden.

The book of Genesis describes the temptation in the Garden as "... tree was good for food ... a delight to the eyes ... desired to make one wise...." (Genesis 3:6) The Apostle John defines temptation as "desires of the flesh ... desires of the eyes ... pride of life." (1 John 2:16) Knowledge of being completely lost must occur before being rescued.

The Garden temptation created an imperfect Intellect, a *loss of innocence.* Genesis describes it as *make one wise.* John defines it as *pride of life.* Romans 1:28 portrays it as, "Since they did not see fit to acknowledge God, God gave them up to a debased mind to do what ought not to be done."

The Garden temptation created an imperfect Emotion, a *loss of contentment.* Genesis describes it as *delight of the eyes.* John defines it as *desires of the eyes.* Romans 1:26 portrays it as, "...God gave them up to dishonorable passions."

The Garden temptation created an imperfect Volition, *a loss of blamelessness.* Genesis describes it as *good for food.* John defines it as *desires of the flesh.* Romans 1:24 portrays it as, "God gave them up in the lust of their hearts to impurity, to the dishonoring of their bodies...."

Before conversion the human nature is fallen and increasingly flawed; by following Jesus the human nature is rescued and gradually restored.

Conversion transforms Intellect - *restoration of innocence.* "Be wise as serpents and innocent as doves." (Matthew 10:16) Innocence is not ignorance or naïveté. Innocence is choosing to reject vain thinking. A convert knows perfectly well unconverted thoughts but considers them unacceptable.

Conversion transforms Emotion - *restoration of contentment.* "Godliness with contentment is great gain." (1 Timothy 6:6)

Conversion transforms Volition - *restoration of blamelessness.* "So that you may approve what is excellent, and so be pure and blameless for the day of Christ." (Philippians 1:10 ESV)

The message of conversion

Two truths comprise the salvation message: "I am imperfect" and "God is unconditional love." The entire human personality needs awareness of these facts. The message to Intellect is *recollection* of disobedience ("I am a sinner") and *revelation* of a Redeemer ("Jesus died for my sin"). The message to Emotion is *remorse* of waywardness ("I feel bad about my sin") and *romance* of the Savior ("I deeply feel Jesus' love"). The message to Volition is *repentance* of rebelliousness ("I no longer choose to sin") and *resignation* of selfishness ("I will make Jesus my Lord").

The human core senses the *weight of sin* and the *magnitude of love* equally and the result is a transforming implosion. The Holy Spirit takes residence in the human heart and Spirit living is birthed.

A nuclear explosion is different than a nuclear yield. Pressure applied uniformly on all sides of a container of radioactive material causes an explosion. Pressure partially applied causes a crack in the container and a yield of radioactive material. In conversion the message is evenly applied to the human personality and explodes with love instead of cracks with fear. The result is a new and renewing life.

Being converted

"They went out from us, but they were not of us; for if they had been of us, they would have continued with us." (1 John 2:19 ESV)

Some people do not experience genuine conversion. More than feeling sorry, a person needs to recognize wrongness and want change. Recollection, remorse and repentance must work together.

Two Montana teenagers attended a church service, heard about salvation and prayed. Both felt guilty about their lifestyle and sobbed uncontrollably. Both were encouraged to follow Jesus and ask for forgiveness. They left the building feeling clean and happy. One went back to living as before while the other started the transformation journey.

To sense genuine love but not be willing to change is similar to smelling something tasty but not choosing to taste. Until the delicacy is consumed, the food cannot nourish life. Conversion is more than sensing the sweet fragrance of hope. The human nature must fully partake of the life-changing message.

A relationship with God is more than feeling bad about unwholesome living. Experiencing God is becoming "born again; born from above; born of the Spirit."

HIGHLIGHT

In conversion there is death then life. "Truly, truly, I say to you, whoever hears my word and believes him who sent me has eternal life. He does not come into judgment, but *has passed from death to life*." (John 5:24 ESV) The human nature is dead and dying, new and renewed. The goal is becoming like Jesus, the destiny is going to heaven. Human intellect, emotion and volition are involved in conversion; knowing sin, feeling sorry for sin and turning away from sin - knowing His love, sensing His love and deciding to make Him Lord. The result is being born of the Spirit. (John 3:8)

RESPONSE

Have you entered into a meaningful relationship with God? Now would be a great time to make a decision to follow Jesus. Salvation is the journey of a lifetime on the roadway of grace. Having faith in God is not a *perfect* life, but a *forgiven* life. Using your own words, humbly and sincerely ask for forgiveness, for help to move toward Him instead of continuing further away from Him, and for Him to rule and reign over you every moment of every day. He very much wants to hear from you.

Jesus said in the Sermon on the Mount "Beware of false prophets, who come to you in sheep's clothing but inwardly are ravenous wolves. You will recognize them by their fruits. Are grapes gathered from thornbushes, or figs from thistles? So, every healthy tree bears good fruit, but the diseased tree bears bad fruit. A healthy tree cannot bear bad fruit, nor can a diseased tree bear good fruit. Every tree that does not bear good fruit is cut down and thrown into the fire. Thus you will recognize them by their fruits. (Matthew 7:15-20 ESV)

CHAPTER TWO
"Fruit and Gifts"

Scriptures emphasize growing fruit.

John the Baptist said: "*Bear fruit* in keeping with repentance." (Matthew 3:8 ESV)

Jesus said: "Truly, truly, I say to you, unless a grain of wheat falls into the earth and dies, it remains alone; but if it dies, it *bears much fruit*." (John 12:24 ESV)

"You also have died to the law through the body of Christ, so that you may belong to another, to him who has been raised from the dead, *in order that we may bear fruit for God*." (Romans 7:4 ESV)

"Walk in a manner worthy of the Lord, fully pleasing to him, *bearing fruit in every good work* and increasing in the knowledge of God." (Colossians 1:10 ESV)

"The *wisdom from above* is first pure, then peaceable, gentle, open to reason, full of mercy and *good fruits*, impartial and sincere." (James 3:17 ESV)

"The *fruit of the Spirit* is love, joy, peace, patience, kindness, goodness, faithfulness, gentleness, self-control; against such things there is no law." (Galatians 5:22-23 ESV)

Comparing fruit and gifts

Much of the talk about the Holy Spirit focuses on *fruit* and *gifts*. Consider the two words together.

Fruit develops through time. Spirituality does not occur instantaneously but is continually shaped and refined. God has all the time in the world and takes whatever time is necessary to produce *good* fruit.

A gift is given instantly. Using a gift correctly and effectively may require practice but the whole gift is available.

Fruit goes through various stages. A seed is planted, the stem sprouts, the shoot enlarges, the trunk strengthens, the plant blossoms, and the fruit ripens, then comes the harvest. Spiritual character goes through similar developments. No one becomes complete without the normal struggle of growth. Godly character starts small and progresses until there is stamina to handle greater responsibility.

A gift is given in its entirety and is complete. Assembly may be required but all the parts are there.

Fruit is visible. Unlike vegetables, all fruit ripens above ground. Spiritual fruit needs *Son-shine* to gain sweetness.

A gift can be hidden. Gifts may be kept secretively and used exclusively. The ability to use a gift as intended may become lost but recipients control usage.

Known by fruit

Is there any wonder why Jesus reveals the criteria for recognizing a false prophet is their *character* more than a persuasive prophetic *utterance*? No matter how eloquent the speaking, how talented the performance, how pious the appearance, or how supernatural the manifestation, authenticity is recognized by *good fruit.*

People rarely remember a sermon but always remember a lifestyle. Are financial obligations being met? Are they reliable? Are confidences being kept? Are they dependable? Actions genuinely express whether someone is following Jesus.

A popular convention speaker once said, "Don't validate a person's ministry by the gifts of the Spirit but whether they pay their bills and whose spouse they travel with." Examining lifestyle is not judging and believers are to give careful consideration of behavior. Are actions consistent or inconsistent with Scripture? God's word is the judge.

Anyone who claims to follow Jesus demonstrates Christ-centered actions. How convincing a person speaks or even the response that follows does not determine the credibility of ministry. How do they conduct their everyday lives? How do they live when no one is looking?

God judges the world but believers examine the lifestyle of *so-called* believers. "I wrote to you in my letter not to associate with sexually immoral people—not at all meaning the sexually immoral of this world, or the greedy and swindlers, or idolaters, since then you would need to go out of the world. But now I am writing to you not to associate with anyone who bears the name of brother if he is guilty of sexual immorality or greed, or is an idolater, reviler, drunkard, or swindler—not even to eat with such a one. For what have I to do with judging outsiders? Is it not those inside the church whom you are to judge? God judges those outside. 'Purge the evil person from among you.'" (1 Corinthians 5:9-13 ESV) These instructions can only be fulfilled by making observations and rendering decisions.

Lives are examined by *character* traits, not cultural *customs.* (Romans 14:1-12) My wife was raised in a very legalistic church. The women wore dresses with sleeves down to the wrist, never cut their hair, wearing it in a bun, did not use makeup, and avoided the use of jewelry. These *customs* are not a measurement of spiritual formation. What if a women who wore long-sleeve dresses, never cut her hair, never used makeup and never wore jewelry was a busybody, gossip, slanderer or liar? These *character* issues measure spiritual formation.

Some quote, "Therefore you have no excuse, O man, every one of you who judges. For in passing judgment on another you condemn yourself, because you, the judge, practice the very same things." (Romans 2:1 ESV) The verse addresses *hypocrisy* more than judging. Others argue, "Touch not my anointed ones, do my prophets no harm." (1 Chronicles 16:22) The verse is against wishing someone *physical injury*, not against observing character.

Many sincere followers of Jesus become captivated by powerful demonstrations of the Spirit, rightfully thinking "Awesome!" A Spirit manifestation, however, is not a measurement of character. Conclusions about a believer based solely on supernatural phenomena lead to tragic consequences. Jesus said, "Do not judge by appearances, but judge with right judgment." (John 7:24 ESV)

Signs and wonders are meaningful and lasting

when accompanied with good fruit. Be leery of people knowing pious clichés yet deceitfully scheming. Some appear flawless on stage yet fail in faithfulness, self-control, kindness and goodness. Followers of Jesus are to live integrated lives, as people of integrity, and align themselves with others of similar nature.

Comparing the fruit and gift of the Spirit

The fruit of the Spirit deals with natural attributes; the gift of the Spirit deals with supernatural manifestations.

Abundant living involves both the fruit and the gift of the Holy Spirit. The *supernatural* is only effective when the *natural* is healthy. They serve as counterweights, keeping a believer upright and steady.

What is cancer? An imbalance of multiplying cells! The *gift life* without fruit and the *fruit life* without gifts causes imbalance, affecting spiritual vitality. Followers of Jesus should not be only people of *power* or people of *polish,* but *polished* people who manifest *power* by the same Spirit.

Secondly, Holy Spirit fruit inwardly develops people to reflect the natural attributes of Jesus. Holy Spirit gifts outwardly manifest the supernatural nature of Jesus. The supernatural power of Jesus was validated by His inward qualities. Power manifested through corruption destroys instead of builds.

Thirdly, reflecting the fruit of the Spirit portrays a *developed* nature and manifesting the gift of the Spirit shows a *yielded* nature. The fruit of the Holy Spirit remodels people in Christ and the gift of the Holy Spirit leads people to Christ. Fruit designs the dwelling place while signs and wonders authenticate the salvation message. Fruit gives a silent witness; gifts give a visible witness.

Growing good fruit

At conversion the fruit of the Spirit becomes implanted in the fertile *soul* as a seed, having nine qualities: love, joy, peace, patience, kindness, self-control, gentleness, goodness and faithfulness. Failing to feel different does not negate that something has occurred. Growth takes time, goes through stages and must be cultivated. The initial change is often small. Wholesome attributes unable to be achieved in the old nature start becoming possible. As the seed grows, abundant life becomes more realized and is expressed as more love, more joy, more peace, more patience, etc. Some results are dramatic and others are gradual.

The seed needs healthy inspiration by lots of exposure to *Son-shine* and plenty of moisture from *heavenly reign.* The seed also needs cultivation, becoming stronger by resistance and toil. The result is *good* fruit. A failure of character is not a lack of possessing good fruit-bearing seed. Bad fruit is not God's fault. Unhealthiness is caused by applying unwholesome influences. Proper care produces godly character.

Homesick for heaven

Followers of Jesus sometimes get "homesick for heaven," especially those with a longstanding relationship with Him. Heavenly homesickness is linked to fruit development. Spiritual formation in this lifetime becomes fully realized in heaven. Holy Spirit fruit planted at conversion makes possible genuine love, pure joy, and complete peace. Through spiritual growth the fruit develops and is expressed as greater love, more joy, and deeper peace. In Eternity comes fullness of love, fullness of joy, and fullness of peace. Heaven becomes home, no longer a strange or foreign feeling. By developing Holy Spirit fruit believers become more conformed to heaven then to earth; they move from seed, to ripe fruit, and finally harvest (a heavenly home).

HIGHLIGHT

Living in the Spirit begins at conversion. Becoming "born again" is the birth of Spirit living. There is death then life. You are dead to sin and dying to sinful ways; you are new in nature and being renewed into the image and likeness of God. When the human nature experiences *revelation*, *remorse* and *repentance*, the Holy Spirit takes *residence* in a person's life.

At conversion the seed of Holy Spirit fruit is implanted in the fertile *soul* of the human nature. Growing *good* fruit requires healthy spiritual activity. The fruit of the Holy Spirit is an intricate part of the gift of the Holy Spirit. Fruit is critical for properly handling the gift. Living with wholeness requires both the fruit and gift of the Spirit.

RESPONSE

Believers sometimes say, "I want more peace" or "I need greater joy." These qualities are already planted in the human heart at conversion. Cultivate them! Give the seed nourishment and greater exposure to the *Son*. Followers of Jesus have a responsibility to grow and to reflect good fruit, and then abundantly *benefit* from them.

"I am the true vine, and my Father is the vinedresser. Every branch in me that does not bear fruit he takes away, and every branch that does bear fruit he prunes, that it may bear more fruit. Already you are clean because of the word that I have spoken to you. Abide in me, and I in you. As the branch cannot bear fruit by itself, unless it abides in the vine, neither can you, unless you abide in me. I am the vine; you are the branches. Whoever abides in me and I in him, he it is that bears much fruit, for apart from me you can do nothing. If anyone does not abide in me he is thrown away like a branch and withers; and the branches are gathered, thrown into the fire, and burned. If you abide in me, and my words abide in you, ask whatever you wish, and it will be done for you. By this my Father is glorified, that you bear much fruit and so prove to be my disciples." (John 15:1-8 ESV)

CHAPTER THREE
"Obedient Life"

Three things determine the quality of fruit: internalized nutrients, external elements giving healthy resistance, building strength, and vegetation or weeds growing alongside. Similarly, what molds and shapes character in a follower of Jesus is *spiritual habits* (nutrients), *circumstances* (external elements), and wholesome or unwholesome *relationships* (other garden produce).

Everything effects spiritual fruit development. The seed imbedded in a new follower of Jesus is going to grow. Will it be healthy and resplendent or corrupt and repulsive? The habits believers establish, the choices they contemplate, and the activities they select impact results. Righteous Holy Spirit seed was planted yet improper care and poor nutrients causes corruption. God is not to blame when fruit ends up rotten.

How is a follower of Jesus designed to live? What practices accurately reflects Him and enhances transformation? The practical dimension of fruit development fits into two groups: *obedience* and *faith.*

Obedience brings conformity to righteousness and freedom from addictive sins. Sin is a vicious taskmaster that always causes death. "Do you not know that if you present yourselves to anyone as obedient slaves, you are slaves of the one whom you obey, either of sin, which leads to death, or of obedience, which leads to righteousness? ... For just as you once presented your members as slaves to impurity and to lawlessness leading to more lawlessness, so now present your members as slaves to righteousness leading to sanctification.... But now that you have been set free from sin and have become slaves of God, the fruit you get leads to sanctification and its end, eternal life." (Romans 6:16, 19, 22 ESV) Motivations, ambitions and intentions are either pure or impure, which one will be obeyed?

Faith develops godly habits. "Do you not know that in a race all the runners run, but only one receives the prize? So run that you may obtain it. Every athlete *exercises self-control in all things.* They do it to receive a perishable wreath, but we an imperishable." (1 Corinthians 9:24-25 ESV) Everyone has habits! Are they good? Are they wholesome, making victory possible when the race of life is complete?

Three *obedient* practices foster dependence upon God, providing greater liberty over wickedness.

Baptism

Visible signs mark people as being different. The Old Testament sign of having a marked difference was *circumcision*, the New Testament sign is *water baptism.* Both communicate to others that the person has *entered* into a new standing with God.

Spiritual acts can sometimes take on a meaning of their own. Circumcision eventually became all-important to Israelites, and water baptism has equally served as conversion in many churches. Water baptism does not convey grace but testifies of grace.

Baptism is significant because Jesus commanded the practice. "Go therefore and make disciples of all nations, *baptizing* them in the name of the Father and of the Son and of the Holy Spirit...." (Matthew 28:19 ESV)

When should someone be baptized? What did the apostles teach and do? The book of Acts demonstrates people were to first believe and then become immersed in water. (Acts 2:38; 2:41; 8:12; 9:18, 18:8; 22:16) Commitment to God occurs *before* baptism.

Water baptism has past, present and future significance. Believers *identify* with the death and resurrection of Jesus, *celebrate* the old nature dying and the new nature coming to life, visibly *proclaim* being His follower, and look with *hope* to the future resurrection. Water baptism is the *public* confession of faith, announcing a person has *entered* into a divine relationship. People can start expecting to see good changes.

Does a person need to be baptized to follow Jesus? Baptism is not conversion but for wholesome spiritual growth, baptism is important. The believer is showing outwardly the inward results of faith and is indirectly telling others to hold them accountable. Water baptism signifies the intent to nurture a relationship with God.

Communion

Baptism is a *onetime* occurrence while Communion is an *ongoing* experience. Spiritual life must be nourished, just like physical life. Taking a morsel of food and a small amount of beverage symbolically reminds believers that Spirit living needs nurturing.

Baptism pictures *faith* in Jesus and Communion portrays *fellowship* with Him and others in His community. Baptism is not done every time a wrong is committed but believers examine themselves during Communion, confessing personal sins and willful offenses against others. (1 Corinthians 11: 27-32, 2 Corinthians 13:5, 1 John 1:9) Followers of Jesus regularly need moments of renewal and the Lord's Table is a reoccurring and refreshing divine encounter.

Communion emphasizes oneness, unity and togetherness. The celebration cannot be done with ill-will. The Apostle Paul corrected the Corinthian church because fellowship with the Lord had become broken and relationships with one another were being affected.

Communion is a *remembrance*, a memorial feast, similar to what takes place at funerals. The elements of the Lord's Table memorialize the supreme importance of His sacrifice. Jesus dying for sin takes preeminence over teachings, miracles and healings.

Communion is a *testimony*. "For as often as you eat this bread and drink the cup, you proclaim the Lord's death until he comes." (1 Corinthians 11:26 ESV) Believers are showing that His death has significance for all time, not just at the time of His crucifixion.

What is being testified? Justification, declared righteous; sanctification, declared holy; preservation, given eternal life; ransom, redemption fully paid; propitiation, sins fully covered; reconciliation, peace with God; substitution, Jesus taking the rightful place of sinners; and, glorification, Jesus glorified before the Father.

Communion is time reflecting upon Jesus, confessing personal wrongness and expressing thanks for His love and sacrifice. The atonement has not lost power to cleanse people of sin and restore them to righteousness.

Tithe

"Hear, O my people... I am God, your God.... For every beast of the forest is mine, the cattle on a thousand hills. I know all the birds of the hills, and all that moves in the field is mine. If I were hungry, I would not tell you, for *the world and its fullness are mine.*" (Psalm 50:7, 10-12 ESV)

"Every tithe of the land, whether of the seed of the land or of the fruit of the trees, *is the LORD's*; it is holy to the LORD." (Leviticus 27:30 ESV)

The issue of tithing is, "Who owns what?" Followers of Jesus are *entrusted* with His possessions and give ten percent of its earnings as an act of obedience.

The tithe began before the Law was written, originally done by Abraham, the father of faith. The Law did not initiate tithing but revealed where to bring it and how to apply it. Jesus did not end tithing but expanded the grace of giving, being given without neglecting other acts of charity. (Matthew 23:23) The *maximum* by Law became the *minimum* of Grace.

Giving produces inward thanksgiving and mysteriously relieves unnecessary condemnation, lifting guilt even when done grudgingly. A United Crusade was hosted by a few churches, using an evangelistic team. A family vacation was planned at the conclusion of the event. During the final night of the crusade people were invited to give an offering. Vacation money was in my wallet. Sensing a prompting to give, a long conversation occurred between the Lord and me. I was tired and wanted to get away for some rest and recreation with my wife and children.

I whispered to my wife my thoughts and she encouraged obedience. The debate with the Lord intensified as the offering bucket came closer. The money was given reluctantly. Immediately peace flooded my soul. The act of giving created a mysterious sense of thanksgiving. Spiritual victory replaced mental anguish. I entered spiritual rest, a divine holiday, better than any vacation could have produced.

Two days later I received a gift that was twice the amount given at the crusade. Giving is not a secret formula for getting, yet acting in obedience develops trust and dependence on God. He often honors submission in unexpected ways.

Followers of Jesus should regularly give and never withhold the tithe. Can the tithe be redirected and designated for a specific use? Not without divine consequences! Like givers, leaders have stewardship obligations. Believers release responsibility for the tithe and leaders become responsible, giving an account to God. Eternal rewards are jeopardized by mismanagement.

Eli was a priest of Israel. He had two wicked sons, not knowing the Lord. When the people offered a sacrifice, the sons would plunge a fork into the pan or kettle and take for themselves whatever the fork brought up. "Thus the sin of the young men was very great in the sight of the LORD, for the men *treated the offering of the LORD with contempt.*" (1 Samuel 2:17 ESV)

The people faithfully gave and God judged the priests for their contemptuous act. The Lord should not be denied what belongs to Him because of wayward leaders. When the tithe is willfully withheld, the would-be giver incurs the consequences of leadership. With a misappropriation of funds people prefer to take matters into their own hands but givers are not the ones being robbed. God is robbed and He repays. If mismanagement is discovered demand better accountability but never deny the Lord His resources. Tithing is an obedient act to God.

HIGHLIGHT

Being "born of the Spirit" occurs at conversion. Following Jesus begins and His natural attributes start growing, being nourished by spiritual habits, circumstances and relationships. As the believer becomes more like Jesus, they better represent Him during moments of supernatural manifestations.

Good spiritual growth involves *obedience* and *faith.* Scripture declares that followers of Jesus *obey* His commands, which include water baptism, communion and the tithe. These actions help produce good spiritual fruit.

RESPONSE

Obedience is critical to Spirit living. Good fruit becomes more evident by fulfilling acts of obedience, which is important for naturally and supernaturally revealing Jesus. Express a commitment to obey Jesus through water baptism, communion and the tithe.

"Do you not know that in a race all the runners run, but only one receives the prize? So run that you may obtain it. Every athlete exercises self-control in all things. They do it to receive a perishable wreath, but we an imperishable. So I do not run aimlessly; I do not box as one beating the air. But I discipline my body and keep it under control, lest after preaching to others I myself should be disqualified." (1 Corinthians 9:24-27 ESV)

CHAPTER FOUR
"Faith Life"

The word *discipline* has been negatively modified to mean *punishment*. The term actually means *training that produces a specific pattern of behavior*. First Corinthians describes how followers of Jesus go into rigorous training to effectively run the eternal race. Discipleship requires discipline.

Both "discipline" and "disciple" have the same root. Believers are disciples by their disciplines. The Heavenly Father is training His children with various disciplines to yield "the peaceful fruit of righteousness" (Hebrews 12:11). Discipline is a *good* word.

Living with structure is stabilizing. The unexpected may add zest to life but living in ongoing adventures is unnerving. Adrenalin is a critical body chemical during emergencies but if constantly flowing can damage healthy organs, shortening life.

Greater contentment and more satisfaction are experienced when life has regularity. Anything less is spiritual constipation, causing uncomfortable, unpleasant and often painful consequences. Something normal and healthy can be destructive without routine.

Another word connected to *discipline* is *habit.* People are creatures of habit, some *help* and others *harm.* Habits are not *broken* but *replaced*; practices are *changed* instead of *ended.* Good habits can minimize falling into bad practices. Someone wrote, "The second half of a man's life is made up of the habits he acquired during the first half." Pascal said, "The strength of a man's virtue... is measured by his habitual acts."

Believers need to establish *habits* that are *enjoyed* instead of *exercises* that are *endured.* Trust comes easily when certain activities are done regularly. Anything done 21 times will become a habit. By doing something every day for three weeks, an activity grows to be normal and natural. Are you willing to instill faith-building practices into your life? Four *faith* disciplines foster hope, helping followers of Jesus run the eternal race with endurance.

Scripture

"Do *your best* to present yourself to God as one

approved, a worker who has no need to be ashamed, *rightly handling the word of truth.*" (2 Timothy 2:15 ESV) Look at this verse through the eyes of Tentmaker Paul. The best work done by a tradesman is accomplished when using the right tool skillfully and correctly.

The word *Bible* means "book," the perfect handbook for living. God, the Maker, had a *Maintenance Manual* written to help believers maintain a highly productive life. When instructions from the *Operator's Guide* is ignored people quickly become worn out, broken down and useless.

The *Book* is a weapon. There is an evil one who hates God's children. *Satan* is the chief "accuser" before God. He is called *devil* because he "slanders," and called *Lucifer* because he impersonates the true "Morning Star." Although a powerful antagonist, Scripture records, "He who is in you is greater than he who is in the world." (1 John 4:4 ESV). Satan is troubled when even the weakest believer reads the word of God regularly. The *offensive* weapon for battle with God's enemy (Ephesians 6:17) and the *effective* weapon used by Jesus in the wilderness (Matthew 4:1-11) is Scripture. Followers of Jesus are to follow His example.

The *Book* is a counselor and healer. Scripture is designed to dwell richly within the human personality. When counseled from its pages a peace is produced that rules every decision. (Colossians 3:15-16) When troubled or anxious, the Bible calms the mind and heals the emotions (Philippians 4:6). When weary by the events of life, the word of God encourages the tired soul. (Romans 15:4)

Believers are to live by the *Book*, used more as a tool instead of held as a shrine. When handled properly, without bias and prejudice, the quality of life improves. When used improperly, for personal advantage and selfish gain, it causes injury. Scripture is to be cultivated into the soul and hidden in the heart. (Psalm 119:11)

Prayer

Shortly after High School I enlisted into the Air Force and became trained as a Nuclear Missile Technician. They sent me to Okinawa and later to South Dakota, working on the Mace and Minuteman missiles. The Mace missile was one of the first missiles designed for military use. The primitive guidance system was created by the principle "*it knew where it was by where it wasn't.*" If the missile was not to the left or right, above or below, before or behind, then it must be where it is. Some wonderful truths about prayer are learned by knowing what it isn't.

Prayer is **not** a physical position, not kneeling, standing, bowing or closing eyes. If prayer was a position then limitations would be placed upon praying continuously and regularly. Posture can enhance expressions of prayer but should not be confused with praying. Kneeling expresses submission. Standing expresses respect and honor. Bowing, a vulnerable position, expresses trust. Closing eyes expresses focus. Posture can be meaningful but is not prayer.

Prayer is **not** repetitive phrases. Each day is new and prayer should be current and relevant. Nothing destroys the habit of prayer faster than *stale* praying.

Prayer is **not** pleading to or begging a harsh *Boss*. Prayer does not involve bodily mutilation in an effort to appease an angry God. Torturing the body and destroying the dwelling place of the Holy Spirit does not prove greater devotion.

Prayer **is** tuning into God's wavelength. Talking to God can and should be done anytime and anywhere, day or night. Conversing with God is done better verbally but can be done non-verbally, vocally or silently. A conversation with God involves few words and long dialogue. Speaking and listening to God happens in crowds and when alone.

Charles Allen described prayer as, "An offering up of our desires unto God for things agreeable to His will."[1] The truest end of prayer is *giving* to instead of *getting* from God. Praying is a melting pot, bringing a person into conformity to

His plans and desires.

Love-Offerings

Tithing involves *obedience*, giving God what *belongs* to Him. Offerings involve *faith*, giving *beyond* an obligation. Tithes and offerings are thought to be the same but the motivation is very different. The tithe is rooted in respect while offerings are rooted in love.

Timothy 6:10 indicates loving money produces a variety of evils. Love-offerings combat love of money and demonstrate love for God. When giving to additional opportunities, believers trust God to provide the means to give and communicate to others a message of faith.

There is no rule about how much should be given above the tithe. Scripture indicates the offering should be within income (1 Corinthians 16:1-2) and should be a cheerful decision (2 Corinthians 9:6-8).

The Bible records stories of people exercising faith and accomplishing great things beyond their abilities. Similar opportunities are needed today and love-offerings put faith into action.

Witness

In a court of law a witness communicates to a group of jurors what was personally experienced. People on a witness stand do not memorize and quote law books, nor do they rarely know or fully understand the court system. A witness is being asked to tell their story. What happened? What was seen and experienced? What were the results? Anyone can be a witness, not just lawyers, judges and law professors.

Followers of Jesus testify their personal experience in two ways, as recorded in Acts 2. Peter explained to a crowd the events that had recently taken place and approximately three thousand people considered his statement accurate and credible. (Acts 2:14-41) The group of believers started gathering regularly, encouraging one another with teaching, prayer and worship, and additional believers joined them daily. (Acts 2:42-47) The chapter is referencing *event evangelism* and *relationship evangelism.*

Believers are to tell others their story of transformation, testifying *a clear-cut change in character for the better.* Unwholesome actions of the past come to an end, improper places are no longer attended, inappropriate conversations cease, and the source of transformation is communicated visually and verbally.

Believers also come together to learn about, pray to and worship God, encouraging one another. Those seeking truth gain a desire for God by experiencing believers in a transformation community. A full church parking lot gains attention. Comments have been made, such as,

"The reason I decided to visit the church was because I saw the lot full of vehicles and thought someone might have answers to my questions."

The message of Jesus is communicated by telling others and coming together. Regularly talking to people about personal transforming experiences and attending transformation gatherings help people become aware that having faith in God makes a difference.

These four faith practices should be cultivated into consistent and regular habits. A great outcome of good habits is they occur regardless of mood and can help change sour dispositions. Scripture reading, praying, giving and witnessing, being done faithfully, produces healthy and helpful perseverance.

[1] Allen, Charles L. *God's Psychiatry*. Grand Rapids: Baker Publishing Group, 1953.

HIGHLIGHT

God's plan involves fruitfulness, not barrenness. Believers are to grow *good* fruit, in other words, cultivate *wholesome* character.

Three *obedient* disciplines and four *faith* disciplines nourish the fruit of the Holy Spirit. Additional activities can also enhance the image and likeness of God. Richard J. Foster in his classic book Celebration of Discipline - The Path to Spiritual Growth considers *meditation, simplicity, confession,* and *fasting* as habits that also aide Spirit living.

RESPONSE

Like obedience, faith is critical to Spirit living. Express faith in Jesus by developing the habit of Scripture reading, praying, giving and witnessing. Active endurance is made possible through acts of faithfulness.

"For you were called to freedom, brothers. Only do not use your freedom as an opportunity for the flesh, but through love serve one another. For the whole law is fulfilled in one word: "You shall love your neighbor as yourself." But if you bite and devour one another, watch out that you are not consumed by one another. But I say, walk by the Spirit, and you will not gratify the desires of the flesh. For the desires of the flesh are against the Spirit, and the desires of the Spirit are against the flesh, for these are opposed to each other, to keep you from doing the things you want to do. But if you are led by the Spirit, you are not under the law. Now the works of the flesh are evident: sexual immorality, impurity, sensuality, idolatry, sorcery, enmity, strife, jealousy, fits of anger, rivalries, dissensions, divisions, envy, drunkenness, orgies, and things like these. I warn you, as I warned you before, that those who do such things will not inherit the kingdom of God. But the fruit of the Spirit is love, joy, peace, patience, kindness, goodness, faithfulness, gentleness, self-control; against such things there is no law. And those who belong to Christ Jesus have crucified the flesh with its passions and desires. If we live by the Spirit, let us also keep in step with the Spirit. Let us not become conceited, provoking one another, envying one another." (Galatians 5:13-26 ESV)

CHAPTER FIVE
"Repairing Human Nature"

Conversion is becoming like Jesus. The message of salvation is "I am imperfect" and "God is unconditional love." When the human personality becomes fully impacted by the *repulsiveness* of sin and the *redeeming* love of Christ, the Holy Spirit takes *residence.*

The personality of the Holy Spirit is not separate from the nature of Christ. Scripture reveals the Holy Spirit expresses inspiration, passion and resolve. He guides believers to *think, feel* and *obey* like Jesus, helping them *discern* good, *desire* good and *decide* good, resulting in *doing* good.

Galatians lists "works of the flesh" and the "fruit of the Spirit," the word "works" being plural and "fruit" being singular. The wrongful activities of the sinful nature conflict and contend with one another for mastery, leaving people fragmented.

The fruit of the Spirit integrates the inner-being and brings wholeness, producing integrity. Instead of subtracting from one another the natural attributes of Christ contribute to the overall beauty and richness of character.

The nine qualities of Holy Spirit fruit easily divide into three groups of three, finding expression through Intellect, Emotion and Volition. As they grow and develop, the human personality is being recalibrated with innocence, contentment and blamelessness. All the qualities find expression in every area but show dominance in one. Well-developed fruit refines and brings believers closer to the original design.

Divine qualities for Intellect

Intellect is the ability to reason, perceive and understand. People of faith do not throw out their *brains* at conversion. Being spiritual does not mean becoming goofy. A relationship with God does not end the use of *gray-matter*, something fearfully and wonderfully made by Him.

Knowing the Lord is an invitation to experience refined thinking. Living by faith may be mysterious but is reasonable. Common sense is God given and inspires faith. The general practice of reasoning should not be discarded in the everyday affairs of life.

People have the ability to distinguish and

know right from wrong, good and bad. The sinful nature is prone more toward calculating, craving and choosing the wrong way, naturally looking for reasons to commit unwholesome acts. Greed and selfishness seem more reasonable than giving and servitude. Scripture states, "Do not be conformed to this world, but be transformed by the *renewal* of your mind...." (Romans 12:2 ESV) The Holy Spirit changes thinking patterns.

Goodness, kindness and peace refines *discernment.*

Repairing *evil* thinking is *goodness.* "Do not be overcome by evil, but overcome evil with good." (Romans 12:21 ESV) "Whatever is true, whatever is honorable, whatever is just, whatever is pure, whatever is lovely, whatever is commendable, if there is any excellence, if there is anything worthy of praise, *think about these things.*" (Philippians 4:8 ESV)

Repairing *cruel* thinking is *kindness.* Kindness means being sympathetic and merciful, thinking the best of others. Of all God's creatures, people treat their own with great cruelty and can be morbidly obsessed with scenes of horror. "Be kind to one another, tenderhearted, forgiving one another, as God in Christ forgave you." (Ephesians 4:32 ESV)

Repairing the *troubled* mind is *peace.* The brain was not originally designed for evil, causing wicked thoughts to haunt the soul. Robbed of tranquility, God implants divine peace. "*Peace I leave with you*; my peace I give to you. Not as the world gives do I give to you. *Let not your hearts be troubled....*" (John 14:27 ESV) "And the *peace of God*, which surpasses all understanding, will guard your *hearts* and your *minds* in Christ Jesus." (Philippians 4:7 ESV)

The fruit of the Spirit restores righteous innocence to the Intellect.

Divine qualities for Emotion

Emotion, how people feel, is the expressive side of the personality. Failing to live for God leads to dissatisfaction, sometimes causing emotional instability. Life produces overwhelming frustrations, creating devastating feelings of disappointment. A relationship with God is the doorway to a happiness that overrides momentary happenings.

Love, joy and gentleness refines *desires.*

Repairing *fearful* feelings is *love.* The opposite of love is fear, not hate. Love and hate run *parallel*, making it easy to jump from one to the other. "There is no fear in love, but perfect love casts out fear." (1 John 4:18 ESV) Love *combats* hate and *casts* out fear.

Fear consumes every part of the human personality. *Intellectual* fear is manifested as *guilt*, *emotional* fear as *anger,* and *volitional* fear as *unruliness.* "For God gave us a spirit not of fear but of power and love and self-control." (2 Timothy 1:7 ESV) There is divinely-given *power* to overcome guilt, *love* to overcome anger, and *self-control* to overcome unruliness, abolishing the products of fear.

Repairing *sorrowful* feelings is *joy.* Pleasant feelings are experienced when entering a personal relationship with God. Every part of human personality is impacted at conversion and people can expect feeling satisfied when following Jesus. The joy of the Lord gives strength over the many sorrows of life. "Your sorrow will turn into joy ... and no one will take your joy from you." (John 16:20, 22 ESV)

"And the ransomed of the LORD shall return and come to Zion with singing; everlasting joy shall be upon their heads; they shall obtain gladness and joy, and sorrow and sighing shall flee away." (Isaiah 51:11 ESV) Believers bandage the wounds of sorrow with the divine garment of joy until groaning ends and a sweet melody of praise returns to the soul.

Repairing *harsh* feelings is *gentleness.* Harshness is feeling good about hurting others, being unpleasantly crude, abrupt, offensive and unfeeling. Gentleness is the ability to be uncontentious and considerate. "A soft answer turns away wrath, but a harsh word stirs up anger." (Proverbs 15:1 ESV) The best intention, without gentleness, destroys.

"Do not let your adorning be external ... but let your adorning be the hidden person of the heart with the imperishable beauty of a *gentle* and quiet spirit, which in God's sight is very precious." (1 Peter 3:3-4 ESV)

The fruit of the Spirit restores godly contentment to the Emotion.

Divine qualities for Volition

Volition is the act of willing. Intellect distinguishes between alternatives and responds, "It appears reasonable." Emotion expresses mood and responds, "It feels appropriate." Volition, however, produces the action.

Volition struggles with the issue, "What do I want?" and has the greatest challenge conforming to the image of God. The Intellect discerns the best course of action yet Volition may choose another. Intellect says, "This is the best way." Emotion says, "The other way feels better." Volition acts partly on what is known and what is felt, sometimes leading to internal struggle.

The Apostle Paul describes an inner conflict involving Volition: "For I do not understand my own actions. For I do not do what I want, but I do the very thing I hate ... For I know that nothing good dwells in me, that is, in my flesh. For I have the desire to do what is right, but not the ability to carry it out. For I do not do the good I want, but the evil I do not want is what I keep on doing ... For I delight in the law of God, in my inner being, but I see in my members another law waging war against the law of my mind and making me captive to the law of sin that dwells in my members." (Romans 7:15, 18-19, 22-23 ESV)

Patience, faithfulness and self-control refines *decisions.*

Repairing an *impetuous* or reckless volition is *patience.* People naturally act impulsively, proceed quickly and tend to be rash, reacting more than acting. Many pleasures associated with special events are connected to anticipation. As people become older they discover enjoyment is partially found in the *waiting interval,* as well as the *fulfillment.* "Patience inherits the promises." (Hebrews 6:12)

Repairing an *unreliable* or undependable volition is *faithfulness.* People normally avoid or hesitate getting involved and can be generally undependable. Living for eternity, however, demands faithfulness. "Be faithful unto death, and I will give you the crown of life." (Revelation 2:10)

Matthew 25 records an illustration of three servants. Two received a response of being *good* and *faithful,* while one received the response of being *wicked* and *slothful.* Unfaithfulness is closely associated with laziness.

"One who is faithful in a very little is also faithful in much, and one who is dishonest in a very little is also dishonest in much. If then you have not been faithful in the unrighteous wealth, who will entrust to you the true riches? And if you have not been faithful in that which is another's, who will give you that which is your own?" (Luke 16:10-12 ESV)

Repairing an *unruly* or rebellious volition is *self-control.* The Holy Spirit does not take control but helps people control themselves. He is called Comforter, Helper, Counselor, Teacher and Guide, not controller. People are always accountable for their actions. A developed volition reflects self-control. The Apostle Peter states self-control is an important part of walking the pathway to His eternal kingdom. (2 Peter 1:5-11)

The fruit of the Spirit restores pure blamelessness to the Volition.

HIGHLIGHT

Upon conversion a person becomes adopted into the family of God and receives the indwelling presence of the Holy Spirit. The nine qualities of Holy Spirit fruit begin to grow and the believer is better able to reflect the *natural* attributes of Jesus.

Becoming like Jesus is the goal of salvation. "We all, with unveiled face, beholding the glory of the Lord, are being transformed into the same image from one degree of glory to another. For this comes from the Lord who is the Spirit." (2 Corinthians 3:18 ESV) The qualities of Holy Spirit fruit work in harmony with one another, showing the *character* of Christ.

A believer's habits and practices provide the spiritual nutrients that grow good fruit. *Obedience* fosters dependence upon God and establishes freedom from wickedness. *Faith* fosters hope in God and establishes endurance. Bountiful fruit ushers in abundant living.

RESPONSE

Followers of Jesus are to cultivate the qualities designed for men and women at creation. The nine qualities of Holy Spirit fruit restore innocence, contentment and blamelessness. Ask God to recalibrate the calculating, craving and choosing dimensions of your heart, which determines the final course of life.

"He presented himself alive to them after his suffering by many proofs, appearing to them during forty days and speaking about the kingdom of God. And while staying with them he ordered them not to depart from Jerusalem, but to wait for the promise of the Father, which, he said, 'you heard from me; for John baptized with water, but you will be baptized with the Holy Spirit not many days from now.'" (Acts 1:3-5 ESV)

CHAPTER SIX

"Spirit Baptism"

The disciples already believed in the Lordship of Jesus (John 20:28) and experienced the indwelling of the Holy Spirit (John 20:22) but were instructed to remain (literally, "*made to sit down*") until receiving the baptism in the Holy Spirit. A short time later, at a Pentecost festival, a special phenomenon occurred involving a supernatural manifestation. With a decision to follow Jesus comes the *indwelling presence* of the Holy Spirit, a believer should then seek to experience the *Spirit baptism*, an additional gift of unmerited favor.

At the outpouring to Jews (Acts 2:38) and the outpouring to Gentiles (Acts 10:45) the baptism in the Holy Spirit is referred to as "the gift of the Holy Spirit." The Holy Spirit is *the gift*, involving supernatural manifestations of grace. (1 Corinthians 12:7-11)

Holy Spirit fruit has nine expressions, while the Holy Spirit gift has nine manifestations that display the *supernatural* nature of Jesus. Acting in harmony with one another, the manifestations reveal the majesty of His might. When a healing, word of knowledge, prophecy, or any sign is witnessed the focus is not on a particular activity but on the supernatural presence of the Spirit.

General differences between a fruit and a gift were compared in chapter 2. Some additional distinctives relate to the fruit and gift of the Holy Spirit.

Holy Spirit fruit reveals the *character* of Jesus and the gift reveals the *charisma* (grace) of Jesus.

Holy Spirit fruit shows the *natural* attributes of Jesus and the gift shows the *supernatural* nature of Jesus.

Holy Spirit fruit *reflects* the purity of Jesus and the gift *reveals* the majesty of Jesus.

Holy Spirit fruit is about *strength* and the gift is about *power*. Having power without strength is abusive. Attempting to power-lift and hold up a 1000 pound barbell without developing physical strength is crushing. Similarly, to exercise the gift of the Holy Spirit (power) without developing fruit (strength) causes extreme damage. Character flaws, a deficiency in fruit development, quickly abuse the gift. The power of God is to be handled honorably.

Three questions are frequently asked involving the Pentecost experience known as the baptism in the Holy Spirit.

Who are Pentecostals?

Pentecostals are *people* of God, abiding in the *presence* of God, manifesting the *power* of God to fulfill the *purpose* of God. Each part of the statement is significant: People of God, *followers of Jesus*; abiding in the presence of God, *living in sincere, honest and truthful worship*; manifesting the power of God, *exhibiting the gift of the Holy Spirit*; fulfilling the purpose of God, *carrying out the assignment to "make disciples."*

The purpose of the Pentecost experience is recorded in Acts: "But you will receive *power* when the Holy Spirit has come upon you, and you will be my *witnesses* in Jerusalem and in all Judea and Samaria, and to the end of the earth." (Acts 1:8 ESV) "Receive power" - the *dynamic* ability, contained in the Holy Spirit, to verbally and non-verbally communicate the message of Jesus. "Be my witnesses" - the *complete* ability to live a life of total and sacrificial service ("martyr" comes from the word translated "witness").

The fullness of the Holy Spirit is a life of faith and service with absolute dependence upon God. He empowers believers to overcome obstacles hindering them from effectively fulfilling the assignment given to the church.

Pentecostals are not just highly emotional followers of Jesus. They seek a divine transformation, *character* change, more than reformation, *behavioral* change. The American penal system illustrates the difference. Confinement is largely based on *reforming* a prisoner from a life of crime with the aid of education and is seeing limited results. Greater results are being witnessed when criminals experience a change of heart, a spiritual transplant. The *transformation* imparts an ability to end a lifestyle of crime.

A high emphasis on a *cognitive* awareness of God is rooted in reformation; a higher emphasis on an *experiential* awareness of God is rooted in transformation. Pentecostals, while having high regards for scholastic achievement, recognize education and training as only one slice in the full realm of experiencing God.

What is the baptism in the Holy Spirit?

The word "baptism" means *immersion.* In the Pentecost experience the believer becomes uniquely engulfed with the presence of the Holy Spirit. After being converted within, the believer can seek becoming empowered throughout.

Many followers of Jesus not recognizing the baptism in the Holy Spirit have effective ministries by virtue of Scripture knowledge, on account of suffering or out of a refined prayer life. Dedicated believers have accomplished much for God. How much *more* could be accomplished through the *full* provision given to implement His assignment? The baptism in the Holy Spirit gives *additional* power and ability, causing *greater* works to be done. Those who have experienced Pentecost should give closer attention to Scripture knowledge, the role of suffering and a rich prayer life, while those denying the experience would benefit by giving closer attention to this additional blessing of grace.

Dr. Gordon Anderson, president of North Central University, describes Spirit baptism in the following manner: "The baptism in the Holy Spirit is an experience with God, subsequent to salvation, in which significant *additional* power for life and ministry are communicated. The experience is characterized by a deep sense of the immediacy of God's presence. By virtue of this, a deep sense of mystery and emotion are often experienced. It is characterized by speaking tongues which establishes a direct super-rational communication with God by means of a language which the speaker has never learned and cannot understand. This experience results in many things in the life of the Pentecostal believer, including *added* faith in God, *increased* power and gifts for ministry, *increased* emotion and passion, and an *enhanced* awareness of the experiential dimension of God's presence."[2]

The baptism in the Holy Spirit has a significant role in fully revealing Jesus to others.

What is Speaking in Tongues?

The book of Acts shows an initial evidence connected with the baptism in the Holy Spirit. Spirit *manifestations* are revealed in First Corinthians and baptism *evidence* is discovered in Acts. Evidence may not have been a problem in the Corinthian church and, therefore, not addressed in the letter written by Paul. Acts shows the experience was evidenced with "speaking in tongues." (Acts 2, 10, 19)

Why *tongues*? The tongue is the most *unruly member* of the human body (James 3:6) and reveals the heart (Matthew 15:18-19). Speaking in tongues is giving evidence of a life being fully *yielded* to God, demonstrating dependence on Him instead of personal resourcefulness. Believers do not *have* to speak in tongues but *get* to speak in tongues.

Speaking in tongues restores what Babel took away, a universal and unifying way of communicating with God. The experience is entering into edifying communication with God in a different way than normal, *heart-to-heart* instead of *head-to-head*, and is personally beneficial. Praying in a known and unknown language builds and strengthens every aspect of Spirit living. (1 Corinthians 14:2, 14-15)

Scripture records absolute liberty is available in the Spirit. Included in this freedom is an escape from the cognitive dimension of conversing with God into a super-rational ability. Unfortunately, personal bias, cultural peer-pressure and family pride has unduly deprived people of this blessing.

"For all the promises of God find their Yes in him. That is why it is through him that we utter our Amen to God for his glory." (2 Corinthians 1:20 ESV) Jesus promised, "And behold, I am sending the promise of my Father upon you. But stay in the city until you are clothed with power from on high." (Luke 24:49 ESV) An important and significant aspect of Spirit living is a more passionate approach to life and ministry, experienced in the fullness of the Holy Spirit.

[2] "Baptism in the Holy Spirit, Initial Evidence, and a New Model," by Dr. Gordon Anderson, President of North Central University, Paraclete, Fall, 1993.

HIGHLIGHT

Conversion is being "born of the Spirit" and leads to developing Holy Spirit fruit. Bearing good fruit reflects the *natural* image of Jesus. A lifestyle of dependence upon God (obedience) and hope in God (faith) provides the spiritual nutrients for sound character.

The gift of the Holy Spirit comes by way of the Spirit baptism and manifests the *supernatural* nature of Jesus. Holy Spirit fruit provides *strength* to properly handle the *power* associated with the gift. Jesus clearly warns that false prophets use the *power* of God for *personal* gain rather than for the intended purpose of fully communicating the way to eternal life. (Matthew 7:15)

RESPONSE

Seek to be baptized in the Holy Spirit. Tangible evidence is given when experiencing the gift. Being drenched with water gives evidence of water baptism and speaking in an unknown tongue gives evidence of Spirit baptism. Ask the Lord to immerse you into the fullness of the Spirit.

"Truly, truly, I say to you, whoever believes in me will also do the works that I do; and greater works than these will he do, because I am going to the Father. Whatever you ask in my name, this I will do, that the Father may be glorified in the Son. If you ask me anything in my name, I will do it ... the Spirit of truth, whom the world cannot receive, because it neither sees him nor knows him. You know him, for he dwells with you and will be in you ... But the Helper, the Holy Spirit, whom the Father will send in my name, he will teach you all things and bring to your remembrance all that I have said to you." (John 14:12-13, 17, 26 ESV)

"But when the Helper comes, whom I will send to you from the Father, the Spirit of truth, who proceeds from the Father, he will bear witness about me." (John 15:26 ESV)

"When the Spirit of truth comes, he will guide you into all the truth, for he will not speak on his own authority, but whatever he hears he will speak, and he will declare to you the things that are to come. He will glorify me, for he will take what is mine and declare it to you. All that the Father has is mine; therefore I said that he will take what is mine and declare it to you." (John 16:13-15 ESV)

CHAPTER SEVEN
"The Holy Spirit"

Fully embracing the nature and ministry of the Holy Spirit is sometimes referred to as "Full Gospel." The baptism in the Holy Spirit and speaking in tongues should **not** be the *Sole Gospel.*

Why do some believers spiritually excel beyond many who recognize the Pentecost experience? When any follower of Jesus gives attention to only one aspect of spiritual formation, they can end up deficient in other transforming qualities. A meaningful relationship with God is more than just Bible knowledge, or prayer, or relationships with others, or character development, or supernatural manifestations, or any single dimension of Spirit living. Every component, when working in harmony with one another, brings spiritual depth and advancement.

Who is the Holy Spirit? What is known about

the Third Person of the Holy Trinity? Understanding His nature increases an appreciation for the empowerment He provides.

The person of the Holy Spirit

The Holy Spirit is not an object or a thing but a Person. Scripture reveals He thinks, feels and does willful acts. The Greek gender for the word "Spirit" *(pneuma)* is *neuter* instead of masculine or feminine, the proper pronoun being "it." Both the Apostle John and Paul, however, refer to the Holy Spirit with the masculine pronoun "Him," emphasizing He is a Person and not just an invisible force, inner attitude or personal disposition (John 16:13-14, Ephesians 1:14-15).

The people of the Holy Spirit

The Holy Spirit has been actively engaged throughout eternity. He was involved in creation and has been operating in the lives of people all through history. He was directly a part of the conception of Jesus.

Uniquely, the Holy Spirit does nothing of or for Himself. He is the *behind-the-scenes* Person of the Trinity. His focus is on the Father and Son being glorified. Without being subordinate to the Father or Son, He delights in directing praise and honor to them. He is Humility personified, helping followers of Jesus to live humbly. In essence, the three Persons of the Trinity are equal;

in actions, the Holy Spirit directs attention to the Father and Son.

To address the sin problem, the Father initiated the answer, the Son provided the remedy and the Holy Spirit applies the solution. Jesus said, "I will send Him to you," (John 16:7) and also said, "I will ask the Father, and He will give you another Helper." (John 14:16) He comes to equip believers for life and ministry.

When the Charismatic renewal was in its zenith years, conferences were hosted emphasizing the Holy Spirit. Songs were written giving special attention to Him. Did He come to be lifted up? The Son of God is Savior, having died on the cross and making possible eternal life. Signs and wonders manifested by the Holy Spirit demonstrate the grace of God as revealed by Jesus.

First Corinthians 12 shows the interaction between Jesus and the supernatural activity of the Holy Spirit. The chapter begins by stating, "...no one can say, 'Jesus is Lord,' except in the Holy Spirit," (v.3) and then gives attention to the church as the embodiment of Christ. From the Holy Spirit comes supernatural ministry (vs. 1-11), unity (vs. 12-20), harmony (vs. 21-26), and the inner-workings of His body (vs. 27-31).

When the churchman Peter healed a lame man, the Holy Spirit manifested the healing power and Jesus received the glory (Acts 3). The Holy

Spirit is revealing the Lordship of Jesus in and through the church.

The power of the Holy Spirit

The church is divinely influenced in three significant ways.

God provides *mentors* to teach and train followers of Jesus. “And he gave the apostles, the prophets, the evangelists, the shepherds and teachers, to equip the saints for the work of ministry, for building up the body of Christ.” (Ephesians 4:11-12 ESV)

God also naturally *motivates* members to harmoniously function in the body of Christ. “For as in one body we have many members, and the members do not all have the same function, so we, though many, are one body in Christ, and individually members one of another. Having gifts that differ according to the grace given to us, let us use them: if prophecy, in proportion to our faith; if service, in our serving; the one who teaches, in his teaching; the one who exhorts, in his exhortation; the one who contributes, in generosity; the one who leads, with zeal; the one who does acts of mercy, with cheerfulness.” (Romans 12:4-8 ESV)

“As each has received a gift, use it to serve one another, as good stewards of God's varied grace: whoever speaks, as one who speaks oracles of God; whoever serves, as one who serves by the strength that God supplies—in order that in everything God may be glorified through Jesus Christ. To him belong glory and dominion forever and ever. Amen." (1 Peter 4:10-11 ESV)

Finally, through the Holy Spirit, empowered *ministry* occurs by the church. "For to one is given through the Spirit the utterance of wisdom, and to another the utterance of knowledge according to the same Spirit, to another faith by the same Spirit, to another gifts of healing by the one Spirit, to another the working of miracles, to another prophecy, to another the ability to distinguish between spirits, to another various kinds of tongues, to another the interpretation of tongues. All these are empowered by one and the same Spirit, who apportions to each one individually as he wills. "(1 Corinthians 12:8-11 ESV)

The church is comprised of mentors and motivated members, and the Holy Spirit empowers for greater ministry. In the fullness of the Holy Spirit the supernatural nature of Jesus is manifested, enhancing the efforts of His body. By being filled with the Holy Spirit believers supernaturally reveal Him according to the need of the moment.

Some like to say they have a *ministry of tongues* or a *healing ministry*. What is given is *empowerment* that can be manifested in nine different ways, depending on the need. The gift of the Holy Spirit is the ability to give a dynamic confirmation of

God's grace, as determined by Jesus.

Be filled with the Spirit

Every believer is to supernaturally reveal Jesus through the various manifestations of the Holy Spirit, increasing glory to God's name and enhancing fulfillment of God's will. "It was declared at first by the Lord, and it was attested to us by those who heard, while God also bore witness by signs and wonders and various miracles and by gifts of the Holy Spirit distributed according to his will." (Hebrews 2:3-4 ESV)

Service to Jesus is based on God-provided motivation, trained by God-provided mentors and empowered for supernatural ministry in the Holy Spirit. The world needs a full revelation of Jesus, which the church is dynamically able to do. Jesus said, "Truly, truly, I say to you, whoever believes in me will also do the works that I do; and greater works than these will he do, because I am going to the Father." (John 14:12 ESV)

A complete witness of Jesus includes reflecting His character and revealing His power. In the fullness of the Holy Spirit believers can fully give the Good News to others.

HIGHLIGHT

The church has been provided mentors to develop members who have unique ministry motivations. The gift of the Holy Spirit empowers believers for more effective ministry in and through the Body of Christ. Service to Jesus is based on gifted motivation, trained by gifted mentors and enhanced by the gift of the Holy Spirit.

Jesus is the Good News. Those who follow Him are to live in *conversion* (relationship with God), *wholeness* (reflecting His likeness), *empowerment* (revealing His nature) and *duplication* (repeating His story).

RESPONSE

Every Spirit-filled believer can supernaturally reveal Jesus. Followers of Jesus should discover what motivates them, allow church leaders to mentor them and ask the Holy Spirit to supernaturally empower them to address momentary needs with divine grace.

"If I speak in the tongues of men and of angels, but have not love, I am a noisy gong or a clanging cymbal. And if I have prophetic powers, and understand all mysteries and all knowledge, and if I have all faith, so as to remove mountains, but have not love, I am nothing." (1 Corinthians 13:1-2 ESV)

"Pursue love, and earnestly desire the spiritual gifts, especially that you may prophesy." (1 Corinthians 14:1 ESV)

CHAPTER EIGHT
"Supernatural Manifestations"

First Corinthians 12 through 14 is about transforming ministry. Becoming baptized in the Holy Spirit is plunging into His presence and being fully engulfed with His nature. With this experience nine dynamic supernatural manifestations become operational. (1 Corinthians 12:7-11) They address momentary needs as He determines and, like everything else in God's kingdom, are exercised by faith.

Similar to *fruit* expressions, *gift* manifestations can be divided into three groups of three associated with Intellect, Emotion, and Volition. The *fruit* of the Holy Spirit restores innocence, contentment and blamelessness to the human personality. The *gift* of the Holy Spirit, *through* Intellect, Emotion and Volition, manifests supernatural *insight*, *inspiration* and *intervention*. The human personality is not overridden but empowered with the Holy Spirit.

The Bible is the recognized inerrant, infallible and inspired word of God. Forty writers were involved with only one Author. The personality of each writer is evident, revealing the Lord worked through people to record Scripture. Just as God worked supernaturally through Spirit-anointed writers to establish His written word, He works supernaturally through Spirit-filled believers to manifest the living Word.

Insight through Intellect

One insight manifestation is an "utterance of wisdom." Wisdom includes *practical skill in the activities of life*. The Holy Spirit gives supernatural clarity to handle a particular situation. The term *utterance* denotes time and place, beginning and end. The manifestation operates in a particular setting and for a specific duration.

Acts 27 records an early church testimony. Three Holy Spirit manifestations occurred when Paul was on a ship to Rome. An *utterance of knowledge* was given to not set sail from a certain harbor, not heeded by the ship's captain. In the midst of a storm *prophecy* was given about no loss of life. Finally, an *utterance of wisdom* came for shipmates and passengers to eat and strengthen themselves for what was about to happen. Three *different* manifestations on three *separate* occasions came through the *same* person.

Believers should not rely on supernatural wisdom when understanding can be acquired naturally. While attending college a final exam was being administered in a Sociology class. A student was asked to lead in prayer before the class took the test. He prayed, "Bring back to remembrance those things we studied and for those who didn't study, what can I say?" An utterance of wisdom is not designed to help unprepared students take school examinations. Acquire wisdom by every available means. When the need can only be met supernaturally the Holy Spirit gives a helpful word.

Another insight manifestation is an "utterance of knowledge." Through the Holy Spirit comes *the supernatural utterance of facts which were not learned through natural efforts.*

Acts 5 records an early church testimony. Peter said, "Ananias, why has Satan filled your heart to lie to the Holy Spirit and to keep back for yourself part of the proceeds of the land?" (Acts 5:3 ESV) Peter received supernatural knowledge about Ananias attempted cover-up and his lie was publicly disclosed, causing the church to deepen their reverence of God.

The final insight manifestation is "to distinguish between spirits." Through the Holy

Spirit comes an ability to *know supernaturally what is motivating a person or situation.* It is the *police investigator* of the spiritual realm, discernment in the cosmic level.

The human spirit, the Holy Spirit, and an evil spirit are three possible sources of activity. This sign and wonder reveals the unseen cause in a given situation. The natural ability to detect and say, "I sense you are unhappy," or "I sense you are uncomfortable," is a developed attribute and is not supernatural.

Acts 16 records an early church testimony. A young maiden was following Paul and Silas for days shouting they were servants of God. Paul discerned the spirit behind the confusion and brought supernatural deliverance to the girl, causing a riot and leading to imprisonment. This supernatural manifestation often intensifies conflict.

Distinguishing between spirits is for spiritual warfare, in order to aggressively attack any evil influence. Not every person coming into a believer's life is sent by the Holy Spirit. The instruction given to the church is, "Beloved, do not believe every spirit, but test the spirits to see whether they are from God, for many false prophets have gone out into the world." (1 John 4:1 ESV) Think well of everyone but beware of deceiving *snakes* lurking about. While sensitive to the Holy Spirit, followers of Jesus do not need to look for demons or evil influences. Concentrate on God and worship Him freely, knowing He will make known when things are out of order.

Inspiration through Emotion

One inspiration manifestation is "prophecy." Through the Holy Spirit comes the *supernatural spontaneous utterance to build up, to comfort and to instruct.* On the day of Pentecost, recorded in Acts 2, the prophetic utterance of Joel was fulfilled. Prophecy is now being expressed through "sons and daughters" of the Lord.

Acts 21 records an early church testimony. Agabus had earlier prophetically prepared the church for a famine. He now tells believers what is going to happen to Paul in Jerusalem. They thought the prophecy was given to spare Paul but he knew God's will. The prophetical word was given to guide believers in their prayers for him, giving Paul the necessary strength to fulfill God's plan.

The next inspiration manifestation is "tongues." Through the Holy Spirit comes the ability to *speak in an unknown language.* First Corinthians 14 mentions several blessings connected with the ongoing experience of speaking in tongues. People are not speaking to others but to God (V.2) and are edifying themselves (V.4). The experience is for everyone (V.5). There are many kinds of languages and all have meaning (V.10).

Praying in tongues is spirit praying (V.14). Believers should both sing and pray with the mind and with the Spirit (V.15). The Apostle Paul regularly spoke in tongues (V.18).

Acts 19 records an early church testimony. Believers in Ephesus had experienced conversion and water baptism. The Apostle Paul visits and recognizes a deficiency in their spiritual formation. After further investigation, he discovered they lacked the means for greater encouragement in the Lord. They were baptized in the Holy Spirit and spoke in tongues.

The final inspiration expression is "interpretation of tongues." The Holy Spirit makes *rendering the tongues, known as glossolalia, understandable to the audience in their language, producing profit.* To interpret does not mean to *translate.* The focus is on the meaning of the *sign and wonder.* Speaking in tongues is a sign, giving conviction about the presence of God, not convincing people of the reality of God.

An example of a related interpretation is recorded in Daniel 5. The king treated the utensils of God's temple with contempt. A hand mysteriously appeared and wrote a message on the wall in an unknown language. Daniel interprets the *sign*, revealing the meaning behind the occurrence, instead of giving a literal translation.

The three inspiration manifestations led to

contention in the early church and can be just as controversial today. First Corinthians 12 lists nine manifestations and chapter 14 gives additional instruction for the ones designed specifically to inspire. Worship gatherings had become chaotic and confusing. The church was told "the spirit of the prophet is subject to the prophet" and worship was to be done decently and orderly. Occasionally people become overly zealous and out of order. Anything touched by the human nature can be abused.

Manifesting the gift of the Holy Spirit is learned and people learn best from their mistakes. Church leaders mentor believers to genuinely exhibit the Holy Spirit. Mentors are the individuals on the court of superstar players wearing the striped shirt and possessing the whistle. They call the time-outs and fouls, safeguarding the integrity of the game. Respecting game officials is how players stay on the playing court.

Inspiration manifestations should naturally occur in worship gatherings, directing praise to God by convicting non-believers and transforming believers. (1 Corinthians 14:22) Sometimes they happen after singing. The Old Testament records prophetic utterances occurring after music was performed. At other times they happen after an exhortation of Scripture, confirming and encouraging a response.

Inspiration manifestations often get accused of being an expression of emotionalism. Many fail to understand that they flow through human emotion and passionately express the grace of God.

Intervention through Volition

One intervention manifestation is "faith." Divine faith! Through the Holy Spirit comes *a sudden supernatural surge of faith, usually in crisis, to believe without doubt in the presence and power of God.* This is *God's faith* for a particular need that no one can add to or subtract from.

Different kinds of faith exist that act on the unseen as if it were so. The Bible records the following: *measure of faith*, given to all; *saving faith*, making someone a child of God; *historical faith*, since it happened in the past, there is confidence it will happen in the future; *ministering faith*, enabling someone to fulfill service for the Kingdom of God; *faith in God*, enabling a person to believe God for something; *faith of God*, receiving divine faith in a unique situation.

Acts 3 records an early church testimony. When going to the temple Peter reached out with supernatural faith and lifted a man lame from childbirth. His legs became strengthened when he stood to his feet. A manifestation of divine faith met the need.

Another intervention manifestation is

"healing." Divine healing! Through the Holy Spirit comes *the supernatural curing of injuries, handicaps, and diseases without the aid of natural means or human skill.* Through Jesus' sacrifice on Mount Calvary comes the provision for healing.

Acts 9 records an early church testimony of healing. Peter was traveling when he came to the town of Lydda. A man named Aeneas had been bedridden and paralyzed for eight years. Peter said to Him, "Jesus Christ heals you!" and he immediately arose. After years of no activity God completely restored the use of legs without physical therapy.

The last intervention manifestation is "miraculous powers;" Divine miracles! Through the Holy Spirit comes an *event that overrides or contradicts the laws of nature.* The principles of probability are God's customary way of doing things. He can change the way things are done, revealing His sovereignty.

Acts 9 also records an early church testimony of miracles. Peter continued his journey to Joppa after healing Aeneas. A woman devoted to serving God had died. Upon entering the room where her body was laid, he said, "Arise." She opened her eyes, saw Peter and sat up. The Lord overruled the laws of nature and manifested His authority over life and death.

Holy Spirit manifestations

All nine manifestations of the Holy Spirit confirm the message of Jesus. Supernatural insight *discloses* God, supernatural inspiration *declares* God and supernatural intervention *divulges* God.

Nourish the spiritual life with wholesome nutrients so that good Holy Spirit fruit grows. Have the strength to handle correctly divine power. The empowerment of the Holy Spirit is not a toy for entertainment but a tool for advancing His story. Jesus fully manifested the Father and believers are to fully manifest Him.

HIGHLIGHT

Today is a day of bondage, sickness and death. Jesus brings freedom, healing and life. By Spirit living, followers of Jesus minister release to captives, healing to the infirmed and life to the perishing. Live in the Spirit and fully represent Him to the world.

EPILOGUE
"The Journey Continues"

One of the unique features of the book of Acts is the way the story never ends. The mission is not over. The church continues telling His story until everyone is aware of the need to place faith in God. The mission will only be fulfilled when followers of Jesus reveal Him in both mannerism and message. Reflecting and revealing Jesus is possible by Spirit living.

The Spirit life is a lifelong journey, requiring lifelong learners. There is much more to understand and experience. The end of this book is the beginning of more faith ventures. The church has received a divine commission to fully represent God and has been given the Holy Spirit to help. Show Jesus to others both naturally and supernaturally.

These chapters were designed to help learn some why's and how's of abundantly following Jesus. The book is not intended to give answers to current challenges or problems being personally faced. The Answer has already been given.

I was privileged to provide leadership to two dynamic churches in the greater Chicago area, ten years in a northwest suburb and six years in a south suburb. The people of Chicagoland are the summit of my calling into ministry. Although no longer living there, my heart and personal burden goes out to this international city, with its numerous problems and amazing people. They are continually mentioned in my prayers.

An older gentleman from the church befriended me shortly after arriving. We regularly went golfing and he told me exciting stories while riding together in a cart. He grew up in a Pentecostal Italian church and kept me spellbound with his many experiences and adventures.

A phone call came telling me he was coming near the end of his life and had been admitted into one of the great teaching hospitals in the area. I went to visit and encourage him. Upon arrival I discovered he had temporarily vacated his room to sit in a busy and crowded seating area, watching people while deep in thought. As I approached he appeared slightly troubled and I asked what was on his mind. He began to relate a dream from the night before.

Jesus appeared and stood before him, looking lovingly at him. He began to ask questions about various experiences that occurred throughout his life, questions about family, career, and personal concerns. Why did a relationship with one of his children go sour? Why did one of his business ventures fail? Why did a partner steal one of his inventions? Why did he occasionally struggle with doubt and fear? To each and every question Jesus simply looked at him and gave no response. As a child growing up in church he was taught Jesus had answers. Why was nothing said to him? Was he unworthy of a reply? Did he do something wrong? He wanted to know what the dream meant and waited for me to say something.

Immediately I sense a divine insight moment. I said, "Jesus does not give answers, He is the Answer. Life will always have questions. Trust Him and walk with confidence in Him." My friend died a few days later, resting in Jesus, the Answer to every circumstance and situation.

Follow Jesus and enjoy the journey designed by Him. Become fully engaged in Spirit living, being led by the Spirit, walking in the Spirit, expressing the fruit of the Spirit and manifesting the gift of the Spirit. The results will be full of wonder.

ACKNOWLEDGEMENTS

Schools: My professors

To Northwest University, Kirkland, Washington, and Southwest State University, Marshall, Minnesota: Thank you for giving me critical tools for experiencing a fulfilling life.

Pastors: My mentors

To Glen Cole: Thank you for teaching the power of truth, with patience and forgiveness, to an unchurched inner-city kid.

To Paul Murray: Thank you for teaching the power of love to a young Airman.

To Albert Knudson: Thank you for teaching the power of sacred music to a young churchman.

To Doyt Allen: Thank you for teaching the power of the Spirit to a young college graduate.

To Ron Masters: Thank you for teaching the power of grace to a young minister.

Staff: My team

To the ministers and administrators that worked alongside of me: Thanks for meaningful and enjoyable staff meetings and for fulfilling each assignment with excellence. Together much was accomplished and sharing the load gave buoyancy to the burdens.

Friends: My encouragers

To Paul Martin, Steve Warner and Larry Griswold for your sincere and close friendship: Together we fought many battles valiantly, bled some, cried a little and laughed a lot.

Family: My strength

To my parents and siblings: Although church was not a part of the home, the foundation of love and loyalty was firm. I always hoped to witness the family following Jesus but they chose not to reveal their final decision. When I go through "the valley of the shadow of death," I long to see them on the other side. Until then I rest in the words of Abraham, "Shall not the Judge of the whole earth do right?"

To Brenda, my especially creative wife and helpmate: Thank you, babe, for the vigilant prayers and steadfast love for me and our family. I stole you from the Dakota prairies and you became a metropolitan lady plus a world-class traveler.

To our children, Nikole, Nannette, Zachary and Stephen: No father could be more thankful for the decisions you have made, the lives you now live and the people you have become.

To our extended children Ryan, Ryan, Shellie and Stephanie: Brenda and I are grateful for you being in the family. You have brought completion to the home and additional viewpoints to the discussion table.

To our grandchildren Skylar, Samuel, Benjamin, Maxwell, Nathaniel, Haley, Lucas, Frankie Jane and Maverick: You give me hope for the future.

ABOUT THE AUTHOR

Bob was raised in the inner-city of Seattle, started attending church as a junior in high school and joined the US Air Force after graduation during the Vietnam War. While stationed in South Dakota he met his bride and sensed a call into ministry. After completing college he entered church ministry with the Assemblies of God, serving in Montana, South Dakota, Minnesota, North Dakota and Illinois.

Bob presently devotes his time to writing, singing and speaking, publishing a weekly blog at bob-maddox.blogspot.com. He is also a nationally accredited volleyball coach, utilizing the high school classroom and a fast-action game to help students develop important *winners-for-life* skills. Moving his ministry into the marketplace has allowed him to better reflect and reveal Jesus to young people in circumstances similar to his past, searching for meaning and purpose while not being raised in church. He passionately desires to see every generation enter into a personal relationship with God and become totally transformed followers of Jesus, made possible by the sending of the Holy Spirit.

Bob and his wife, Brenda, raised their four children in the Chicago area. Each child has chosen to devote their lives to following Jesus and to utilize their unique giftings to advance the divine message of hope and change. They now reside in close proximity to some of their grandchildren in Ozark, Missouri.

ACTION, Reflections from the gospel of Mark
"Introduction"

Years ago I read an article from an Episcopal priest about various kinds of churches, mentioning their strengths and weaknesses. He started with liturgical churches, transitioned to mainline churches, moved to evangelical churches and ended with Spirit-filled churches. He believed they collectively contributed to the final mosaic of the Church.

When looking at the Spirit-filled church he complimented them for their emphasis on the blessing of the Holy Spirit and for elevating, as people of faith, the importance of the supernatural. He then stated a great weakness is in not knowing Jesus. He considered them anemic in understanding the gospels and, with all of their talk about the Savior, did not know Him very well.

The indictment caused me to examine my own reading habits of Scripture. I had to admit my study of the New Testament centered mainly on the writings of Paul. I was lax in regularly looking at Matthew, Mark, Luke and John and committed myself to do an aggressive reading of the books. I started by examining a Harmony of the Gospels, two times successively. After looking at the book of Acts, Luke's gospel being a two-volume edition, I studied each gospel narrative individually. The Episcopal priest was right, I did not know Jesus. I was telling others about someone I did not comprehend very well.

Some scholars are presently calling themselves "Red-letter Christians," referring to the statements of Jesus being printed in red by some Bible publishers. Although not a part of this group, I attempt to read through the entire Bible yearly and give the Gospels an additional reading.

The first three New Testament books, known as the *synoptic* gospels, show the life of Jesus from a parallel point of view. As a teenager reading the Bible for the first time, I wondered why Matthew, Mark and Luke similarly recorded the same events. The three writers give an accurate account of Jesus, viewing Him from different perspectives and describing Him to distinct audiences. The fourth gospel, John, is a bonus feature that plays an equally important role.

My wife and I through the years have enjoyed looking at new homes, gleaning floor plan and decorating ideas. Occasionally while driving we come upon a newly built house and stop to peak through the windows. By viewing the same room from different windows, we see things slightly different. Correspondingly, by looking in all the gospel *windows* a clearer picture about the life and times of Christ becomes revealed.

In my earlier years of following Jesus the four gospels were simply history books, written to give general facts and information about the Son of God. I did not recognize the divine benefits from reading stories of things occurring centuries earlier. A college professor expanded my perspective. The Apostle John indicates not everything Jesus did was recorded. The gospels include carefully selected stories. The historical events chosen were designed to help awaken non-believers to the *need* of faith in God and also *increase* the faith of believers.

I started a new habit of praying before reading and studying the gospels, asking for the stories to mold and shape my spiritual formation. While reading I also started asking myself questions: Why was this particular incident recorded? What transforming benefit did this event have to the initial audience and original readers? What in these stories can help me tackle current challenges and situations?

The second gospel writer is thought to be John Mark, the one who accompanied Paul and Barnabas on their first missionary journey. He possibly wrote in the city of Rome, giving descriptions of incidences witnessed by the Apostle Peter and designing the content for Romans, more than for Jews or Greeks. The readers were culturally similar to today, technologically advanced for their era and gleaning knowledge from various customs. He writes a concise account of Jesus to extremely industrious people. The narrative is filled with action, another display of contemporary life. The gospel begins abruptly and proceeds rapidly from one episode to another.

Following Jesus was becoming more difficult around the time of its writing. Some believers were being treated cruelly. Torture was on the increase and death was not out of the question. Mark, inspired by the Holy Spirit, wrote a stirring account of the life, suffering, death and resurrection of Jesus. Described for believers in every generation is the *Perfect Standard* for experiencing hardships and facing difficulties.

ACTION, reflections from the Gospel of Mark, emphasizes at least one incident from each chapter, showing a relevant application for today. *If it happened to Jesus, it can happen to you - if they did it to Jesus, they may do it to you.* The life of the Anointed One shows how to handle both the ongoing and unexpected stresses of life.

[Coming Winter, 2014]

Made in the USA
Charleston, SC
09 May 2013